About the Author

Adaina is originally from Liberia, on the west coast of Africa. Her writing is her way of communicating with the world. Her interest in writing started when she became so lost in her own broken shattered pieces. Writing made it easier for her to express herself, and when her imagination comes knocking, she makes sure to use her special key to open and welcome it with open arms and write what millions of us feel, but don't dare to say. She specializes in short stories and poems.

Well, Mama, This is It
(It's Now or Never)

Adaina

Well, Mama, This is It
(It's Now or Never)

Olympia Publishers
London

www.olympiapublishers.com
OLYMPIA PAPERBACK EDITION

A CIP catalogue record for this title is
available from the British Library.

ISBN: 978-1-80439-658-2

This book is a memoir. It reflects the author's present recollections of
experiences over time. Some names and characteristics have been
changed, some events have been compressed, and some dialogue
has been recreated.

First Published in 2024

Olympia Publishers
Tallis House
2 Tallis Street
London
EC4Y 0AB

Printed in Great Britain

Dedication

I dedicate this book to all the teenagers who find it difficult to express themselves. I dedicate this book to all the men and women living secret lives. Last but not least, I dedicate this book to myself. Yes, to myself. Writing this book helped me realize that my words become clear when my mind awakens.

Acknowledgments

I thank God for his wisdom and knowledge, and special thanks to myself for believing that anything is possible, like I always say, "Having a free mind allows you to speak without your mind being imprisoned."

The Words of a Teenage Boy

To Grandma, Roselina

How are you doing? I hope all is well with the entire family. I miss everyone so much, especially my favorite pet, Bobo. I'd also like to thank you for the early birthday gift. I love it! And I sincerely apologize that I won't be celebrating my special day with you all this year. A lot has been happening in my life, and I have been quite busy steering my life in the right direction. It has not been easy, but well, I'm surviving and moving on strong. Moving away from home and into the big city has been quite challenging, but it has also helped me see and understand life differently. And although high school life is hard, it's full of new experiences to remember. I am now physically active because of sports and outdoor adventures. High School is full of fun and unforgettable moments, and the best part about High School is that it's full of all kinds of people. Vittra High School has the popular rich kids, the shy and nerdy kids, the gay and proud, the kids that are playing God's role of judging everyone, and then the hiding-in-the-closet kids, because they were raised in a Christian household, and are afraid of getting disowned. Isn't it funny and exciting how one school can have so many different individuals? Life is full of different categories of people, Grandma. And sure, we may not always agree with their choices in life, but we can try to see and understand them for who they are. And finally, we must love and treat people with deep respect regardless of their social status.

P.S. Life in High school has opened my eyes to see the world in a whole new way, and I just wanted to share my experiences with you on this crazy journey that I am on.

My deepest love and kindest regards, I wish you all a wonderful month.

Signed, Leo.

Exploring, Hustling, and Experiencing

Description: In the hope of making some quick and easy money, achieving high success, and owning the finest things in life, I went from working as an elementary school teacher to becoming a stripper.

Rapsan (Lady of the night)

A Story of a Friend of a Friend

I worked as an elementary school teacher for almost two years. Then I made the decision to quit and started working as a stripper. I desperately wanted to have a luxurious lifestyle. I felt I had the looks, body as toned as a fitness instructor, glowy skin as a goddess, lips ripe as cherries, and eyes that could capture anyone's attention. My friend Mia always told me I had the "Look" to be on the front cover of every magazine, and I honestly believed her. I thought it was about time I got out there to explore the beautiful dream cities and live my fantasies. I began searching for strip clubs and pimps. I was doing almost anything I could to get noticed.

Then, after four months of hard work, I finally got the telephone call I had been waiting for. It was Jason Ringa, the owner of the JR strip club, to whom I had applied a few months earlier. JR, as everyone called him, excitedly told me that I was fit and gorgeous enough to be one of his girls. That got me smiling and giggling like a nervous schoolgirl. As the conversation progressed, we agreed to meet for a tour of the building.

On a Friday at twelve forty-five p.m., Mia and I met JR at his club. He seemed very polite and tried his hardest to get me to understand my schedule and get familiar with the place. Being in the strip club physically made me feel as though I had gotten a big movie role from a popular, well-known director in Hollywood. I felt so happy and proud and thought I was about to start doing something fantastic. I just couldn't wait to get home to call Mama and Dada (my stepfather) knowing my parents, I knew they wouldn't be as supportive. Mama always told me how naive I was, and I never questioned her statement. I had one dream and one dream only, and that was chasing money. Coming from a lower-class family, getting rich for me was my number one priority. I wanted to go from rags to riches within the blink of an eye. Seeing how hard Mama and Dada work to provide for our family, I just wanted to take that burden off their shoulders. I imagined what life would be like getting away with almost anything without any consequences, experiencing the politician's lifestyle (money talks, bullshit walks). I wanted my family and I to live in the suburbs just like in the movies and have the finest house on the block.

Well, as for Mama, she felt we had the most beautiful life anyone could dream of. She was a very simple lady and wasn't about living a fancy life. She always told Dada, "Long life, good health, having a roof over my head, and having the best and most loving husband in the whole world make me the happiest and luckiest woman alive." I will laugh at Mama and tell her she was missing out on the most important things in life. She will respond with, "Money makes you mad, and fame gets you killed." My darling, Rapsan, pray to God to always have your common sense and never forget the introduction to the book of your life. I got goosebumps, and my lips felt numb. I couldn't tell Mama about JR's club. I had the feeling of calling JR and quitting even before starting, but I thought it'd be unprofessional of me.

Two weeks later, at six p.m., I drove down to Adamvills, street number 0808, to meet JR to start my first day of work. I dressed to impress that day. I wore my favorite heels, a French pedicure with colors, darkest black smoky eye makeup with nude lips. I felt drop-dead gorgeous. On my first night, I made a very good amount of money, including tips given by customers. Well, three months into the job. I had already started missing out on having a normal life. I started regretting being part of this industry. Jesus, I lost count of how many times I had to stay professional and respectful to a bunch of aggressive perverts just for the sake of getting the right amount of money. It's a very unsatisfying and dangerous business. This is not a job for the faint-hearted, and some girls get into this business in the hope of getting discovered by a modeling agency, some lonely millionaire, or a popular rapper. And just like a fairy tale book, you patiently wait in total misery until your prince charming comes along and rescues you. I envisioned the perfect life.

Oh yeah! I dreamt of everything, I dreamt of fancy things and owning it all, but here I am wishing that I could be like you, feeling free and alive. Oh, a little bit of freedom, a little bit of peace, and love is all I need. Oh, how I used to daydream of fancy things and owning everything. Now loneliness has become my only companion, using Hennessey and Ecstasy, to take my shame away. Now, here I am, shamelessly and desperately wishing that I could be like you, feeling free and alive. Because a little bit of freedom, a little bit of peace, and love is all I need.

Quote: "Strippers, prostitutes, and adult film stars are often looked down upon in society, but the truth is that we don't know what they go through when the lights go off, and they are left alone with their thoughts."

Second Chance at Life

A fresh start: After losing my dignity and my self-worth, I made the decision to accept my mistakes. With the right attitude to move forward, I returned to teaching. Taking a deep breath, I felt truly alive. Witnessing these beautiful moments, life for me now is exactly how it was meant to be.

Motivational quote: "Dear friends, having delicious food on your plate, access to clean drinking water, a roof over your head, good health and a loving family is a blessing. I'm not saying money is a bad thing, but making it our number one goal leads to an unsatisfied life that sends us to an early grave. Be kind to yourself, take small steps, and strive to have a more peaceful, fulfilling, and happier life."

Secret Agent (Voodoo Princess)

Description: Work of my imagination. Rebecca Tanon, an undercover agent. Ability: Feeding on the souls of the innocent.

"Our innocence gets taken away from us at times, but that's because we are incapable of standing up for ourselves."

Rebecca Tanon is the daughter of Mr. And Mrs. Tanon. When Rebecca was born, it was the happiest moment of her parents' lives because the only sadness they had experienced was not having a child. Luckily for them, God blessed them with one. Due to her parents' tradition and their desperation to become rich and own over twenty properties, they made a deal with a voodoo priest. The voodoo priest promised to give them power and make them the richest people in the world, as long as they were willing to sacrifice their unborn child, someone whose fresh blood would satisfy the devil.

They had agreed to sacrifice their daughter before she was born, and once they gave birth to her, she automatically became one of the devil's disciples. Abandoned by her family, who were unable to care for her. Rebecca grew up knowing she had power and how to use it. Due to her special ability, she could see people invisible to human eyes. When Rebecca was ten years old, she was introduced to a stranger as her biological father. As a result, she directed her anger towards those around her, becoming very aggressive and completely fearless. She spoke to older people in an unpleasant manner. She could attack almost anyone because she had people protecting her. These people were like her family, and the dark world was their paradise. They were like slaves, and they had to obey their master and live up to his expectations. Rebecca was a confused child growing up; she couldn't make her own decisions without her followers. She was brought up to believe that her only achievements in life were to get married and become a housewife before reaching a certain age because it was their tradition. When Rebecca was sixteen years old, she got into drugs and prostitution, and soon became a young participant in the sex business. However, that was her way of getting closer to her victims. There were so many dangerous, demonic thoughts going through Rebecca's mind. She felt like giving up on life and disappearing from the universe. But she couldn't escape because her parents had arranged a marriage for her with Mr. Doonate in their dark world before she was even born.

The only way Rebecca could live on Earth as a normal human being was for her to become an undercover agent. From that day on, her mission began, and she was left alone to face the world with great power. But, as we all know, "With great power comes great responsibility" Rebecca was told not to return to the dark world, referred to as "Paradise," until her mission on Earth was accomplished. When Rebecca first became an undercover agent, her mission was to make human sacrifices, which included killing innocent people. A few years passed, Rebecca changed her looks, dressed in clothes that were unlike her, and went to lots of parties. She started smoking and drinking heavily, becoming the typical country girl in the big city. During that time, she met her first love, Joshua Thompson, whom she later broke up with. Nobody was too good or powerful for her. She provoked, tempted, entered into, and transformed herself. She enjoyed manipulating and controlling people, making many turn against each other. She manipulated police officers, caseworkers, and friends. Rebecca Tanon was very careful not to reveal her true identity to friends and caseworkers. She went around making people believe that she was an innocent girl who needed help, but deep down, she was a living demon who was on a mission to destroy people's lives. The devil knows your name and every move you make. They try to destroy your desire to live a holy life and try to make you worship them. Their greatest temptations are towards "good people," not liars, thieves, and murderers. Because they already control them.

Wishing you all health, wealth, love, and happiness in the new year ahead.

As we approach the New Year (2023), I'd like to rewind on the past years, most especially the year 2020. It was a year that will not be easily forgotten.

We were all excited when the year 2019 ended and couldn't wait to see what the new year would bring us. Some of our family members couldn't wait to start new jobs, some families had weddings, baby showers, and gender reveals planned, and tourists were excited to travel around the world to see beautiful countries and learn about different languages and cultures.

Quote: "The world and cities are meant to be seen. We can't stay in one place forever."

But as the saying goes, no one knows tomorrow.

What I'm trying to say is that we can imagine and plan out our lives, but at the end of the day, our entire lives lie in the hands of God. He knows the beginning and the end of each individual on this earth.

In 2020, we were hit hard by the deadly pandemic, COVID, which took millions of innocent lives. Some of us had to struggle even more to provide for our loved ones. The strong, confident, motivated husband turned into a weak, lost, worried, depressed, and hopeless husband. His thoughts began to manifest into reality, "What am I going to do now? Am I still the man of the house? Do my wife and children still see me as the best husband and father in the world? How much longer will this madness continue? Do I have the strength to face another day?" (Suicidal thoughts.)

These are not just the thoughts of a man, a father, or husband, but the thoughts of our mothers, sisters, brothers, uncles, aunties, children, nieces, cousins, nephews, grandparents, musicians, authors, actresses, junior high school/university students, and ourselves.

(I don't think anyone could predict what the year 2020 was all about.)

A psychic or a preacher cannot predict our future or when we will depart from this world. If we have issues,

We take it to the church

and give it to the good man upstairs

because he knows what's best for us.

He knows what rocks our world.

God knows our worth.

Since I have talked about things that happened in 2020, I would like to talk about an event that happened to me.

True Story

My Haunted House

Description: The dead do talk, but only if you listen carefully.

As I lay my head on my pillow, I drift off to sleep with my phone on and music playing in the background. I always fall asleep to music from any of my favorite artists. Beautiful music that helps me fall asleep quickly, random videos or series on YouTube, but most importantly, Bible verses for protection while I sleep. This has been a habit of mine for as long as I can remember. As the saying goes in Ephesians 6:12: "For we wrestle not against flesh and blood, but against principalities. The simplest way to put this would be we do not face a physical enemy, but a spiritual one." This saying can only be understood by those who know Jesus Christ, the Messiah. Noticed how I didn't say "Christians" because not all Christians practice what they preach. Some Christians even claim to read the Bible but don't understand what the Bible teaches. Well, readers, allow me to show you a world beyond.

The date was Friday, May 27, 2020. Between one and two a.m. I forgot to say my daily prayer. Whenever I don't pray, I have dreams that are so frightening that they could send chills down my spine (literally). Often, the things that we see in our dreams are God's way of communicating with us, no matter how bizarre it may be. God reveals to redeem. As Africans, we translate and understand dreams differently compared to Western countries. I had a dream that felt real. In the dream, we moved into a new apartment, and as we were setting up our furniture, I could strangely see the familiar faces of people that I once knew. I often dream of these people on different occasions, but what I saw out of the corner of my eye was a glimpse of a little girl, a ghostly figure.

She looked about eight or nine years old, but what was more disturbing was her appearance. She was covered in smoke, as if she had died in a house fire accident. She started wrestling with me, pulling me out of the apartment, screaming loudly and repeatedly, "DON'T SMOKE! DON'T SMOKE!" I tried to respond, but my mouth opened without any words coming out. Feeling weak and speechless in my dream, I was terrified. I couldn't move or turn in the physical world, but I could see myself praying in my dream and asking God for protection. Suddenly, I began to speak.

I wanted to get as much information from her as possible, but, most importantly, explain to her that I don't smoke, not even in my real life. *What was her reason for appearing to me?* I thought to myself. *Was she a messenger, my guardian angel warning me that I was in the wrong place?* As I started to gain strength and make sense of my surroundings, I could see the apartment we had moved into burning down to the ground, with the entire building crumbling. As this ghostly child stood watching over me, she said, "The dead do talk, but only if you listen carefully."

A Personal Letter from the Author

Compliments of the season!

To my loved ones.

It has been a long time since we last saw each other, so I wanted to write to you all during this lovely holiday season. I hope this letter finds you all in good health and that you all are enjoying the best days of your lives during this special time of year. I am doing well and trying to appreciate life by God's grace. I am a simple woman, so I am not having an extravagant celebration this Christmas. I would rather take whatever money I have and buy something practical for those in need. What's new in my life now is that I have changed a lot since you last saw me, adopting a new mindset to grow and be better. Real friends are hard to find, so I keep my circle small. I have also unfollowed certain people to be in control of my life. I observed every person I had in my life, and I figured out who to keep my distance from (as of today, I have frenemies and enemies). As the year is about to end, I am setting new goals for myself for the year 2023. I want to lose a few pounds, eat better, organize my home, and just simply be myself without a care in the world. I just love the person that I'm becoming, and honestly, I LOVE MYSELF. It feels fantastic to say it out loud. In today's society, you have to be your biggest supporter because only you can manifest the life that you want. Always trust and believe in God.

My best wishes to all of you.

Merry Christmas

Merry Christmas and a happy New Year!

May this Christmas bring you all the love and joy you deserve.

Smile and be glad because it is Christmas time.

So, smile and be glad!

Merry Christmas to you and your family

May the blessings of the Lord remain with you, my loves

May all your wishes and dreams come true,

And may the spirit of Christmas bring you love and hope

Smile and be glad because it is Christmas!

Life gave me lemons. I didn't make lemonade, I mixed it with my Holy water and drank it.

Where and how do I start?
It has been a crazy, sad, but exciting year. I am writing this letter from the comfort of my own home. Let's start from the

beginning of the year, shall we? In February of 2021, my boyfriend of one year went to be with the Lord due to cancer. It was a devastating time for all of us, but thanks to my Redeemer, I wore my big girl panties and walked away from that dark side of life. No one knows when death comes, but I must admit that cancer is the biggest serial killer that takes victims of all ages and genders. I wish we could lock it away with the key to the cell door and bury it underground. I will be the first to proudly walk with a protest sign.

Happy heavenly birthday, young soul.

April 2021

Since my boyfriend's death, I have taken it upon myself to visit him at his new home (the graveyard) and continually pray for him. I pray that the good lord accepts his soul and that my darling Zen-Zen is resting in eternal peace.

Yes, he's gone, but not forgotten. He still deserves my love and prayers, and to keep the laughter that we once shared, I made sure to serve him all the juicy neighborhood gossip. I also read out the birthday card that I made for him by hand with lots of red hearts and stars.

"Happy heavenly birthday and happy Easter, Mr. Handsome. Rest easy in Christ's love, as your birthday is the same as his resurrection.
Hugs and kisses, forever yours, Adaina."

A short message to the readers: "There is a time that we go from light to darkness and from darkness to light. It is the universe's way of teaching us that we are not in control of this thing called life."

It's the second half of the year 2021.

July 1st
I went from struggling to get out of bed every morning to now having a passion for life. For once, I feel alive. I never thought

that I could feel this way after Zion's death, but I do! I went from feeling hopeless, scared, and confused to feeling fantastic, brave, and confident. Isn't it crazy how one's life can change in a minute, month, or year? I am a living testimony that it's all God's work. Ladies and gentlemen, now that I have got your attention, allow me to reintroduce myself.

Poems to Grab the Reader's Attention

"Tell me stories
I have never heard before
Make me feel like an angel in the devil's world
Oh, loves
I need someone to lift me up
I need someone to fill my cup
To drink when I'm thirsty
Because, darling, lately, lately
I have been feeling so sick
I need someone to lift me up
Yeah
I need someone to fill my cup."

I believe in you.

They say you won't make it far,
Some say you won't touch the sky,
But I believe in you
Because I know what you can do.
I know that you will break all the rules
That has been set for you.
I will be here for you
24/7,
Baby, I will be your heaven.
No more depression,

No more war.
Baby, I know what you can do.
I hope you know the sky is the limit for you.
I know they say you won't make it far,
Some say you won't touch the sky,
But, darling, I believe in you
And I know you will break all the rules.

Tea

If I could be like all the princesses in my village, I would choose to live a simple life, because it's all I need and it's all I want. I don't have to rush a thing, just doing my thing. In my own universe. The boys are my friends, and the girls are my besties. We are drinking tea and sharing tea, just doing our thing. We don't have to rush anything; we are just living a simple life. A girl downstairs says she's pretty, she's beautiful, and rich, and that's all she really needs. "Oh, I don't really care, I am just here drinking my tea, and doing my thing. It doesn't matter what you look like; if you want to join our team, come and drink some tea and share some tea."

Description: I am not lost, I am not confused, and I am not gay, but I am a woman who has accepted being loved by another woman.

My dearest mama, I never in a million years thought that I'd write you such an intimate letter, but a desperate situation calls for desperate measures. I have hesitated a lot on coming out to you, and that's because I always felt that the time wasn't right, but I know deep within that the longer I wait, the harder it gets on me. I have therefore chosen this particular day (Wednesday) to come out of my closet because I need to drop the weight that is on my shoulders. People always wondered why someone would choose to come out.

Some say it doesn't matter, and then some are so moved by the whole thing.

And that's because when someone chooses to come out, it's a way for them to finally be themselves and hopefully touch one person in the audience to face their fear (whatever that may be).

Well, Mama, this is it. The time has finally come for me to be free as a bird.

Free as the beautiful spring roses and flowers. Let's catch our breath.

Before you continue reading this letter, imagine how life has been for us.

Imagine the beautiful mother-daughter relationship that we have developed over the years.

Imagine all the tears and joy we have shared. Mama, do you remember when I told you I am your number one fan and your biggest cheerleader?

Do you remember when I said I am your assistant and the keeper of your secrets, and how I pray day and night that God blesses me with wealth so that I can take care of you for the rest of my life? That's because you are my favorite person in the whole wide world. There are not enough words in the dictionary to express the love that I have for you, Mama. You have a special place in my heart, which is why my coming out to you matters. I want to know that nothing will change. I want to know that I can continue to be myself when we are having our daily conversation. Throw in a joke or two without feeling uncomfortable or getting an awkward laugh. Before I say what I want to say, I want to acknowledge that it may or may not be an easy pill for you to swallow, and that is perfectly fine. You are allowed to feel whatever emotions take over you, but I don't want you to be hard on yourself. I know you have questions, and you may try to blame yourself for my mistakes and choices, but I want you to know that you have not failed as a parent. My decisions and actions in life have nothing to do with you, Mama. As I'm getting older, I'm learning new things every day, I'm learning about myself (my likes and dislikes), and I am also learning how to cope with the challenges that life throws at me.

"Mama, I never knew love could hurt this much
I'm sitting in my room thinking about how Father left
I know he hurt you
But you have been so strong
Moving on with your life
But somehow, I'm stuck in mine
Oh, Mama, I never knew love could hurt this much
I'm sitting here thinking about how Father left
They say a girl looks up to her daddy
Sorry, Pops
But you are not worth it
Just thinking about how you left your family
To be with Anna Lee
Oh, Father, I'm the one picking up all the missing pieces
Oh, Father, I'm the one fixing all the broken glasses
I'm the one trying to hold everyone together
Oh, Father, oh, Father, I wonder if you know how hurt I am
Trying to hold everyone together
Oh, dear God, I never knew love could hurt this much."

I won't sugarcoat my relationship with my father.

You know the story, and I think the audience has gotten a little insight. Well, Mama, you must be questioning yourself if a child not having a father in their life plays a big impact on who they grow up to be.

The answer is yes and no.

A child not having a father doesn't indicate what the child later becomes in life as they get older. Some children grow up with two parents, the parents are hard-working citizens with no criminal record, who provide whatever the child needs. And that child could grow up to be a rapist and a danger to themselves and society. Take Jeffrey Dahmer as an example. By the way, have you heard of Jeffrey Dahmer? If you haven't already, you should watch the series about him that is streaming worldwide (it's worth watching). I won't go into too many details, but Mr. Dahmer grew up with two parents who tried to raise him into a young man who could navigate his way through life. However, Jeffrey Dahmer was dancing with the devil when no one was around. He danced and danced until the only thing he could see was the reflection of himself as a puppet being controlled by its master, which created so much evil in such a young soul. Jeffrey Lionel Dahmer was an American serial killer and sex offender who murdered seventeen men and young boys.

Yes, Mama, a child can have the best of both worlds and still take the wrong path.

Can a child not having a father in their life play a big impact on what the child later becomes?

Yes, Mama, take me for an example: I won't have a typical wedding

Because I'm not like the other girls

Who gets walked down the aisle by their dada

Oh, Mama

Daddy walked away when I was just a kid

I have managed to live without him

Oh, I have managed to dance without him

Oh, Mama

I know I won't have a typical wedding

Because I'm not like the other girls

Who gets walked down the aisle by their dada. I grew up not knowing what a father-daughter relationship is supposed to be like.

Growing up without a father left me with little knowledge of how a young woman is supposed to be loved.

This led me to look for true love in the wrong places and with the wrong people/men. I walk down the street searching for what I have missed for years.

Hoping to find a man who could love me like a real father loves his daughter

Or a brother loves his sister

And in return, I-I promised to be their lover forever.

I wasn't born this way, Mama. I have been in love with Adam's gender, but I have now accepted that it's perfectly normal to fall in love with Eve's gender. I sometimes question my sexuality and wonder what I should do. I know talking about it could help me process whatever is going through my head, but growing up, I always felt true love for Jesus Christ, our savior. I learned about Christianity from my aunts and uncles, who constantly talked about the Gospel of Christ and what the Bible teaches us. Their favorite topics and lectures were about the Ten Commandments and how sinful it is to be gay, and that God was against homosexuality. I always sat through the entire conversation in total silence and listened. But as time went on, I lost track of who I was and started questioning my sexuality. Oh, Mama, some men, women, and young adults have questioned their sexuality at some point in their lives) "It is perfectly normal as humans." But I never spoke about my feelings, and I always just kept them hidden away from the viewer's eyes. Locked up all inside. Of course, I wish I could have shown those around me how I felt deep inside. God knows how many times I cried myself to sleep. He knows how many times I confessed my feelings.

"Oh, Lord, I've kept this act for so long, I just don't know how much longer I can continue."

Being raised in a Christian home and growing up differently from the rest of the "regular kids" out there. I've never felt so close to anyone to tell them exactly what goes on in my mind and life.

I'm going around in circles because everything now seems like a rollercoaster ride.

LGBT

I am fully aware that society won't accept who I am because fifty percent of the population find Lesbian, gay, bisexual, and transgender lifestyle repulsive:

Pause. Pause… Pause.

I took a break, Mama, because I needed to take a warm bath to help me clear my head. I could write down thousands of words, but I must say that it is not about writing thousands of words; I want the chance to write exactly what I need to say.

I know after reading half of my letter, you must be in total shock and glued to your chair, sofa, or king-size bed.

And asking yourself:

"How could I have missed these signs?"

Why didn't I see that my child was in a world of her own?

Is there anything that I could have done differently to prevent this from happening?

I know and understand exactly how you feel, Mama. It's not always easy to know a person, and this is because family and society have taught a person to wear masks perfectly. We get so used to these masks that we feel completely naked without them.

Let me rewind two years earlier. When I was at the age of eighteen and working as a young secretary, my duties were to answer phone calls, maintain files, and schedule appointments. My favorite part of my job was being able to work effectively with and meet many different individuals. I learned from every single person that I met, and over time, I developed a strong relationship and an ability to communicate with the people I worked with. But I sure wasn't prepared for the transition I was about to face in my life. Everything was just so new, new friends and a new city. After we moved from the east side of Riverlake to Kortcity, and although it was extremely tough at first, time flew by really fast, and I learned to adjust to the new changes. The people we met here were super amazing and have helped us tremendously.

Sexual Orientation

Do you remember that beautiful sunny day in August, with the sky so blue, as we sat on our balcony looking out at the quiet road? You began questioning me out of curiosity about my love life and why I wasn't dating yet. I remember it as if it were yesterday.

"Child, you are beautiful, smart, compassionate, and with unique qualities and personality. I pray you find your prince charming someday."

I said, "Amen," with a smile on my face because we had attended church, and it was made clear to me that homosexuality was a sin. With the ups and downs and confusion in my life, I freaked out a little and didn't know what to say after that. But the truth is that I was silently having a conversation with God, our creator.

"Dear heavenly father, you know everything about me, you have heard my prayers and pleaded for help, and you have also seen my tears and scars. I am in a dark place.

Oh gosh, I'm feeling insane.

Life is so hard

It feels like I'm drowning…

Oh, just how I have cried

Screaming out loud

I'm so lost

I don't know where to go any more."

"Yes, dearest Mama, I know that love is a complicated thing, but I believe that love is love, regardless of gender. Jesus loves us all equally, no matter how big our sin is."

I am in love, Mama, and it's not the type of love that leads me to seek advice from a relationship therapist, radio station, some psychic, or my next-door neighbor. This love has been blessed and renewed by the highest.

"Love is sweet
If you find the right guy
Love is sweet
If you find the right girl
All the clouds will go away
Darkness will fade away
The rains will stop pouring, babe
And you will see beautiful colors
Like the rainbow
Because shawty, you got me feeling some type of way
Ah, yes, love is sweet
Love is sweet, love is sweet
If you find the right guy
If you find the right girl

love is sweet."

"You see this girl right here, Mama
She makes me smile,
You see this girl right here
She's the reason that I'm all right
I'm clean
Oh, I feel so free
Because I said bye to all the Ecstasy
Oh, honey, honey no more Hennessey
Oh, Darling, darling, it feels good to be me (again)
Oh, I can walk with my head held high
It feels so right to be all right
Oh, honey, you are the reason that I'm free
Now, no more monsters chasing me."

"Hey,
My baby got red lips
Black hair
glowy skin
And she shines bright in the darkness
Oh, she's my beautiful diamond
My beautiful diamond
Because when baby laid her healing hands on me
I felt some type of way
Now my life is not the same
Oh, my beautiful diamond, my beautiful diamond
Girl, because of you, because of you
I feel some type of way
Oh, my beautiful diamond, my beautiful diamond
Girl, you are my favorite star

Oh, my shooting star."

I don't have a prince, but I found a queen who treats me like
a princess. We started as pen pals, but she allows me to be myself
without judgment. Our first letter is attached.

"I wish, I wish upon a shooting star
that everyone finds someone
as kind and romantic as you are

Because if they did, the world would be
A happy place filled with thousands of smiles

My sweetheart,
you always find a way to make my day

Thank you, my sunshine, for all you do
These, my words, I say are sincere and full of faith."

"1 2 3
Tell those girls that you belong to me
I have been walking around town
Going in a circle, round and round
Trying to clear my head
To think about the year
That I will say 'I do' to you
When you ask me to be your boo
Oh, baby,
Thousands of words in my head
I can't comprehend
Because when I'm with you

The sky appears so blue
Oh, beautiful baby
My angel,
Is right here, yeah,
Tell those girls that you belong to me
And I will inform the boys that you mean everything to me
Because when I'm with you
The sky appears so blue
And I thank the Lord for bringing you into my life
Because you are my angel,
My freedom."

"Thank you for loving, loving, loving me
Oh, holding, holding, holding me
You see,
I have been loving guys who think I'm mad
And that I'm the reason for everything falling apart
Because they don't know how to love me
They don't know how to hold me
They don't know how to treat a queen, a queen like me
But, darling,
Since the day I met you
My life seems so sweet
And I feel like I can touch the sky
When I'm in your arms.
Oh, baby!
Thank you for loving, loving, loving me
Oh, thank you for holding, holding, holding me."

"Bang bang, I will take out my pistol
Then pull the trigger, bang bang
Girl, I will kill for you, I will steal for you
Heck, I will destroy any fool who tries to trouble you, bang
bang
Girl, we are in it together, we stand together, fight together
Damn, I will do anything to strive with you
I will lay my life on the line for you
Heck, I will fight off any demon who wants to take away
your soul
Because, babe, I won't let you be lifeless with me because
your battles are mine, your worries are mines
Bang bang
We are in it together, we stand together
And fight together."

"Come and pay my dowry
Down here in Kortcity
And take me home to your family
I promise we will live happily
Girl, if you give me a house
I will give you a home
And if you give me your love
I will give you my own
Girl, if you give me a house
I will give you a home
A warm home
And if you give me your love
I will give you my own
So come and pay my dowry
Down here in Kortcity
I promise we will live happily."

To My Newest Pen Pal, Jant Leaps

Hello Jant,

How are you? You may know me as 'Jess', but my name is Adaina. I am originally from Riverlake, born and raised, but my family and I moved to Kortcity. I am a twenty-two-year-old student with a passion for becoming a writer/musician. But life and its unpredictable challenges got to me, causing my mind and soul to freeze for eternity. I was left with just an empty body.

Oh, dear Jant, as I am writing you this self-expression letter with shaking hands, but with a fulfilled, pleased heart. Well, I would first like to say my soul is at ease and happy now, and that my shaking hands are due to my nervousness because of some of the things I'm about to write in this letter. I'd also like to say how thankful I am for having you as a pen pal because after reading your letters, I cannot help but realize how much alike we are, even though we are of different ages. I have also always wanted to speak to someone apart from a psychologist; this is just among my many thoughts, but I think that we sometimes need someone completely different from a psychologist.

You know, someone who has experienced and survived life's difficult challenges that one is experiencing now. I believe psychologists are trained to keep calm during any given situation, and it's their job to try to understand and make you feel better about yourself and whatever you are going through. You are, of course, welcome to give your honest opinion about these thoughts of mine, my darling, Jant. You see, I have had role models in the past who decided to take the easy way out when life gave them difficult challenges that they thought they could not beat.

Oh, Jant. I have felt like this at times, and I think it's because we often doubt ourselves and our capability to do things, and our words and thoughts simply become those of an empty and fearful child. Yes, I too have made some mistakes in the past, and I wish I could have done things differently, but honestly, I have learned from my mistakes, and now I just want to be able to express myself without my mind being imprisoned.

Oh, Jant. I do constantly think about the future and what awaits me, but as for now, I just want peace. I want to experience love from the people who are available to give it. I want to touch the stars before they disappear before my very own eyes. Well, my precious, Jant. I'm almost at the end of my letter, and I'd like to thank you from the bottom of my heart because the best thing about this journey has been having you on my team. You have given me the ability, strength, and confidence to openly write to you and receive nothing but complete love. I often tell myself that love is such a crazy thing, because I don't know how to feel within.

When it comes knocking on my door
So, I tell myself
It's okay
Because my dearest Jant,
When I talk with you
Your voice hypnotizes me
And your words
Keep me falling
Falling for you

So, it's okay
Yeah
I know that I'm safe with you
I know just what to do
When I think of you
So, it's okay
It doesn't matter what they say
It's okay, babe. So
Tell me all your stories
Tell me how you feel deep within
When the light goes off
And everyone lies in their houses
And you are left with all your thoughts
Good or bad
Don't you cry
because
I'm all ears
All yours
All ears
All yours
Lay it down on me
because I have been down this road before
So, I know how to go with the flow
Lay it down on me
Tell me how you feel
When the light goes off
And everyone lies in their houses
And you are left with all your thoughts
Good or bad
My darling, Jant
Don't you cry

because
I'm all ears
All yours
My brothers and sisters in Christ say that dating the same
gender is a sin, they say you are bad for me
You are not the one for me
And you'd make me sin
Oh Jant
They say you are bad for me
You are not the one for me
because you'd make me forget everything I have learned
You are like a bad fire (they say)
And if I touch you
I might get burned (burn to ashes)
My darling, Jant, I don't discriminate
I'm here to stay with you
because the good Lord says
Love thy neighbor
So, I'm here to shower you with love
Oh, Jant, I don't discriminate
I'm here to stay with you
Forever, so
Nothing they say
Nothing they do
Would make me walk away from you
So, darling
Put on your dancing shoes,
Let's hit the dancefloor
And have some fun!
Let's hit the dancefloor.
And let go of all our worries

Shake it away, baby
Let's shake it away, oh baby.
Let's have some fun!
I have bills to pay, but so what?
I'm going to move my hips.
I have rent to pay, but so what?
I'm going to shake my waist.
So put on your shoes, my lady
Let's hit the dance floor
And have some fun.
I am slowly and romantically confessing my love for you
using love poems that I have written especially for you, Jant.
It's true,
Girl, I'm in love with you
There are so many things that I wish I could do for you
But for now
I will look up at the sky
And thank the Lord above all
For all of my blessings and healing
For helping me stand on my feet
Through trials and tribulations
Oh, God is my savior
God is my everything
And when he walks with me
Baby, best believe that I can walk with you
Oh, it's true,
My darling, I'm in love with you
So, tell your mama
Tell your papa
Tell your brother
Tell your sisters

Tell your uncles
Tell your aunties
That I'm the one for you
And you are the one for me
They may not see it
Or believe it
But darling, I'm the one for you
And you are the one for me
I got everything you need
Peace dripping over me
Darling, I'm the one for you
So, tell your mama
Tell your papa
Tell your brother
Tell your sisters
Tell your uncles
Tell your aunties
That I'm the one for you
And you are the one for me
They may not see it
Or believe it
But darling, I'm the one for you
I got love in my heart for you
For you
Oh, peace dripping over me (for you)
So, tell your mama
Tell your papa
Tell your brother
Tell your sisters
Tell your uncles
Tell your aunties

Tell your friends, your best friend
That I'm the one for you
And you are the one for me.

Quote: "Life isn't always about money or materialistic things. It's about showing unconditional support during difficult times and having love and acceptance for one another."

I still remember our conversations as if they happened yesterday. The late-night phone calls, the moments that made me giggle because of how deeply in love I was with you. Do you remember

When I said, "I have what you need, I promise, I will give you the angel number 606, because you are worth it. You know what they say, love makes you crazy. I know you want love, and so do I. So why do you hide? I have what you want, I promise, I will give you 606, because you are worth it."

I never thought I could fall in love with Eve's gender, but there's always that one person who comes into our lives and changes the way we feel and behave. Now I find myself saying:

"I love myself,
Darling, I love you too.
Yes, I love myself,
Oh, darling, I love you too.
because self-love comes from within,
And if I love myself,
Then darling, I love you too.
I am strong, I am happy.

Oh, darling, I feel so free like the beautiful spring roses.
Oh, darling, I feel so free like the birds flying up in the sky.
I feel so blessed to say,
I love myself
Oh, darling, I love you too."

"My darling, Jant. I don't know what the future holds for us,
but I will tell you this: I know it's true love, babe
So, I will never walk away
because it's true love
It's so rare,
Yeah.
It doesn't happen often.
Oh, babe, your love has softened me
In this foreign country
on a beautiful Sunday
Yeah.
I will never trade your love
because what we got is worth fighting for
It's true love,
I will never walk away. Yes, I am a Christian, but my
religion is kindness, my religion is humanity, and love is my
religion. My religion is not to judge, discriminate or hate. I will
fight with you. I want to fight for the people who cannot fight for
themselves. I want to fight for you and me so that we can all live
in a better world. I think of you in silence when I often lie wide
awake at night, when everyone is fast asleep. Remembering all
our beautiful conversations. I remember how beautiful and bright
you truly are, like a summer rose. I imagine what life would be
like with the most beautiful, kind-hearted woman on the face of
this earth. I imagine us living in a two-bedroom and two-

bathroom apartment. I have, of course, never lived with a significant other before, but I guess it could be our way of announcing to the world that we are official. You are my genie in a bottle, granting all my wishes. Everything seems like a dream, and this is because I have never been loved the way that you love me, Jant. I secretly question your intention at times, not because I think you are a bad person, but when a broken heart finds a healer that loves deeply, the whole world becomes a dreamland."

Quote: "We may not fit into the category set by society's definition of what love is supposed to be like. We may get physically and verbally abused by strangers who struggle with their demons in silence. We may get turned away from Church gatherings, but whatever troubles, traumas, or disappointments we may face
Not once or twice, but
a million times
May our love for each other grow as strong as the wind and be as beautiful and as pure as the angels walking amongst us."

"Someday, we will sit on our balcony, sipping real tea.
We will talk about the old days
Oh, we will talk about our days
How we fought hard
To be just where we are.
I promise you, babe, that
you and I
will survive the storm
So don't listen to what they say,
because all they do, babe

Is tell tales
But I promise you, baby
you and I
will rise above the hills.
Yours sincerely, your pen pal, Adaina."

No matter who comes out of the closet, as Christians, protesting "being gay is a gateway to hell" is not going to change someone else's decision to live a lifestyle that they have already chosen for themselves. When someone announces that they are "gay," our mind immediately thinks about grabbing our Bible and preaching the word of God, sharing our beliefs and what we have been taught. I know it's difficult and scary to accept someone who is so different from us, but at one point in our lives, we struggled to accept our own body, mind, and soul.

"Our situation won't always be the same
Because we have the power to make a change
1, 2, 3
Let's get all emotional.
Let's get in touch with our feelings.
Come on, relax with me.
Let's smoke a joint
And connect with our feelings.
There's no need to be ashamed.
So, tell me how you truly feel.
I know they say big girls don't cry,
but, baby, I don't mind.
I will be your shoulder if you want to cry
So lay it all on me now
And share how you feel deep inside."

Quote: "Tell me, young loves,
what is life like for all of you?
Where do you imagine yourselves to be?
Sure, I'm just a country girl,
but I have big dreams too
Sure, I'm just a country girl.
My darlings, I'm just like all of you.
I'm a fighter
I'm a lover
I'm a learner
I'm a teacher to myself,
and someday to someone else (I hope, yeah)
Sure, I'm just a country girl,
but darlings, I have big dreams
And I hope, I hope that my dreams will
Come true."

My mission has always been equality for all, and I just want to encourage and inspire young women and men in our community to be themselves and be their best. The only way I can achieve my goals is to be an example and a good communicator for the voiceless, no matter the circumstances.

With love from Kortcity, Adaina.

When my time comes to depart from this world, I will leave naked, weak, and empty-handed (material things won't matter). The only legacy that I will leave here for the next generations to follow is the love that I share through my writings, the compassion that I showed, the humbleness in my voice, and my gratitude toward life.

"Adaina."